The Art of the Flip:
How to Creatively Succeed in Job Interviews

Kevin J. Parkinson

I0463530

ISBN-13:ISBN-13: **978-1501079863**

Dedicated to everyone who is trying...
God bless you in your effort; don't stop until
you obtain what you want.

CONTENTS

Open

A lot of times we find our self in situations where we cannot express how we truly feel, we don't have the words to explain it. We can't **"Big up our damn self!"** That is a Jamaican term for showing pride in yourself and thoroughly presenting yourself to others. Most popular songs released in the United States are written at a third-grade level to ensure the message can transcend audiences. Not a lot of words past the elementary level are exposed to the masses through popular culture. Sometimes this results into people's inability to communicate in certain settings. Causing several times of grief and frustration.

Today, in Corporate America, in Entry Level America and Small Business America, we all need to be able to explain ourselves and represent ourselves verbally well inside of interviews. Job interviews are designed to be comfortable for the

employer, who only wants to make sure that the weak candidates are thrown out immediately. And why shouldn't they? He or she has the luxury of having 100 others candidates to interview today alone. To do this, he or she is going to give you weird questions that you're going to need to answer well and quickly. Your ability to communicate will be tested and your personality will be sent through the ringer. The only way to be successful in one of today's job interviews is to know the type of questions that will be asked and how to answer them. This book, written by an experienced and awarded Career Advisor, will teach you how to flip questions into favorable answers that positively reflect you as the best candidate for the job. After reading this book you will understand how to represent your brand best, you will master the **art of the flip.**

Chapter One: Overstand

Overstand is a slang found in Rastafarian culture. It breaks down to this: **To understand is to operate a video camera, but to overstand is to know how to design, improve and build the camera.** If you have made it this far into the book but read no more pages, all I ask of you is this. Try your best to Overstand every interview you have. The End. If you are still reading, here is what I mean. Imagine it is 1991, you are on a date, you pull up to their house and they get into your car. The vibe is right because both parties have the same agenda: To have a good date; however, the signals are funny. They told you before that they love comedies, and you suggest that you go see the new Eddie Murphy movie; however they then say, "I don't care what we do." It's raining, so anything outdoors is out, plus this is your on your 4th date, so movies are a fine choice. The Movies make the most sense. **What do you do?** You overstand the situation. What is the person wearing?

How does the person smell? Is the person hungry? Does the person like Eddie Murphy? Are you doing your best to use these understandings to make an educated decision?

You are going to have to overstand the situation because the other person has left you with the power on how to proceed. The same setup goes for all of your interviews. Ask yourself, what type of employee does this employer want? What is the personality type of the best

employee for this job? Does this job require someone who can deliver something I can?   Use the understandings of the job that you have to flip any question asked. Is the employer a funny person? How does this employer dress? What is the tone in the place of business? Is my interview personality presenting me in a way that matches this jobs culture? Does this person have a hand in a cast; should I ease up on my handshake? Overstand, overstand, overstand. Always. Or as my Father would say, "Look around look around." **A great tool is to mimic. Mimic the personality and tone, without being condescending, of the person who is interviewing you.** The object is to not come across as making fun of a person but through subtle body language and tone relate to the other person presence. In Chapter Three: The Physical, we will go over this more in depth.

Chapter Two: The Flip

In different markets, the "flip" can mean different things. In gymnastics, it means human jumps backwards or forwards and makes at least one revolution with their body before landing. In the Housing and Used car market, flipping refers to buying cheap, improving and then selling for a profit. **But I want you to start looking at Job interviews as a market, a market of its own.** Think about it, we buy clothes for interviews, buy bus or train passes and gas to get to interviews. We invest time into using the internet for job research for interviews. A lot of money is spent and made from those looking for or preparing for interviews; **In this market, flipping has to do with making interview questions and answers reflect you positively.** Let's take a simple look at a good and bad flip.

Example 1:
"What is your greatest weakness?"
"I never want to clock out, because of how engaged I become in my work!"

Example 2:
"What is your greatest weakness?"
"I don't have one."

Which answer served the job seeker best? **Funny how an answer that seems strong can be very weak and used against you in an interview.** Let's break down this simple flip. In example number one, the job seeker answers the question by explaining their excellent work ethic. Simple, straight forward and noteworthy to the employer. This person wants to work and work hard. In example number two the job seeker comes off ignorant, here is why. **To not know of your weakness is to not know yourself, to not know yourself is to not have any self-discipline, to not have any self-discipline equates to being an awful employee.**

The interviewer may not even get this deep consciously, but subconsciously the answer puts up a red flag. Someone with no weakness may be un-trainable, unfit to work in a team and unwilling to admit fault. No employer is looking for this type of person. As you can see, the flip is very deep. As rapper Rick Ross once said "It's deeper than rap." Meaning, take nothing for face value, overstand everything happening in any job interview. Especially the questions. Let's try again:

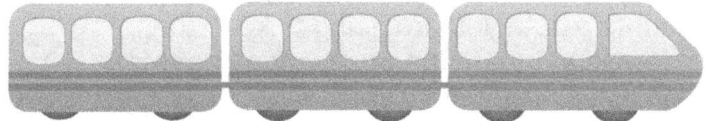

"Tell me about yourself"
"I don't know; I'm just a chill guy."

Tell me about yourself"
"I am a very committed person and I love working on teams."

We already understand why the second answer is a better answer, so let's examine the first answer. **No matter what language is popular in the English vernacular, never use any words you would use when talking to a friend. This weakens you severely.** This answer tells the interviewer nothing about the person being interviewed; It is almost a slap in the face. It is defensive. The interviewer cannot bounce anything off of that answer; the answer stops the conversation and does not add to it in any way. Always progress the conversation. Look at it like this; you are on a date anytime you interview. A date with someone you really like. This person you find attractive, and feel a connection with. If you get the opportunity to date this person, the first time you officially hang out and both understand you are on a consenting date you are going to keep the conversation fun, to the point, engaging and progressive. You both want to find out as much about each other as possible, and you both want to look your best. Let's try one more, this time a bit harder.

"Why do you want to work here?"
I want to work here because your company is one of the biggest companies in North America, and I want to be a part of that. I love the respect you have in the industry, and I want to be on a team that is widely known.

"Why do you want to work here?"
Your company makes the best consumer products that help people with seeing disabilities drive better. Your commitment to the community through your giveaway programs, and discounted products are admirable, the philanthropy you guys show exemplifies that you care about the customer and not just earning a paycheck."

"Why do you want to work here?"
I love the morals this company stands by and the company mission. I feel my skills will best be used here to advance the company and allow me the opportunity to grow within this organization.

So which answer is the best? They go from worst to best. **Understand that the interviewer is looking out for very specific things, they want to learn about your career goals and if they match with the position you are applying for.** No matter if you are in High School student or a professional; They want to know if you're sincerely interested in the position and if you will have the motivation to work hard. They want to know your priorities and why the job is appealing to you. Lastly, they want to know what you know about the company. If this interview was important enough for you to take the time and research? This answer is not about sucking up to the interviewer. They already know if the job sucks or if the position is in a dream organization. No need to fake the funk. Be honest, don't come off as doing anything to gain acceptance in the interview; instead, flip the question into showing off your ability and self-worth. Let's reexamine the "Tell me about yourself" question. Which answers best to flip it?

1. Tell me about yourself
Not much, I'm trying to work here, and I am a parent.

2. Tell me about yourself
I like long walks on the beach and to hike; I surf and develop video games for cell phones in my spare time with my friends.

3. Tell me about yourself
I'm originally from Charlotte North Carolina; I hold a degree from Saint Vincent A&T in business management. I took my last company from a yearly gross of 1.2 million to 3 million, and I love working with teams to collaborate.

4. Tell me about yourself
I am new to the job market; however from my experience as a volunteer and my ability to interact well when working with others I know I can apply my skills to maximize productivity of this organization.

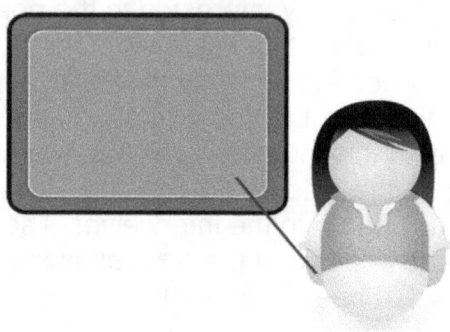

So what was the best answer? Simply put, answer number 1 is way too personal. There is nothing wrong with being a parent; however, it is not an appropriate response to the question since this question is really about you as an employee. Answer 2 is great if you are on a date, not for this question. This person told the employer everything about themselves except what type of employee they are. **Answer 3 and 4 are both excellent answers.** These answers practice the art of the flip. Answer 3 is from a professional that knows their worth and value. The answer stresses past achievements and exposes education. Answer number 4 does the same exact thing. It's hard to realize compared to answer number 3, but the answer is just as effective. **This person knows their worth and value. Self-awareness is a great tool to practice in a job interview.** The words volunteer, experience and skill demonstrate education. Let's go over other commonly asked questions found in job interviews, and how to best answer them.

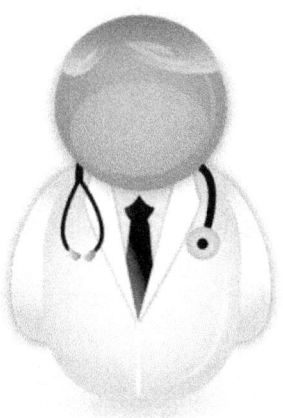

What are your strong suits?
This is a question that allows you to shine really. If you did not answer the question accordingly to what the interviewer was looking for with the last question, use this question's answer to tell them about your work ethic.

How much do you expect to earn in this position?
The best way to deal with this question is to not let it seem that money is not important. If you say a salary that is too little, you will look under qualified and may be offered a lower wage. If you say too high, they will assume no matter what they offer you, it will be turned down. So research the company's wages first and give an educated answer to what you are looking for.

Why did you leave your last position or why do you want to leave?
No matter what happened at your last place of employment, or is happening at your current organization, never bad mouth the job or people there. Again with the dating scenario, a negative person will come across as scorn. A red flag that this person is not ready to date. You naturally put yourself

on the other side of the story when a date has awful things to say about an ex. You start to thing "I wonder what they did to make the ex not want them?" Instead, flip it by saying things like "I am looking for opportunities to grow" and "I want to expand my skills." This shows your initiative, and that you admire the company, you are interviewing with.

Let's try Dual Sided Questions. These sneaky questions are designed to show your bias, do you value one thing over the other? Don't fall for the trick; just flip it into two positive answers about yourself.

Do you consider your customer service skills or technical skills more important?
Your answer should show that you value both of these skills. Do not allow your chances of being hired to be diminished by choosing one. Use the Art of The Flip. Here are some examples to how you can answer this question.

- **I value my technical skills to be able to perform my job well, and I appreciate my customer service skills in that they allow me to assist customers the best way possible.**

- **Both skills are crucial to maximizing the productivity of my organization.**

Which is more important to you in a job, fulfillment or pay?

Both pay and compensation are important. Answering only one way will look foolish. You cannot stay at a job that makes you miserable but pays you well for long. And you cannot afford to stay at a job that underpays you even if it brings you much joy. Let's look at good answers that will allow you to look honest and competent.

- **I feel that in order for an employee to be most effective at work, he or she must be paid adequate wages for the work they perform. That way there productivity is highest.**

- **Both are equally as important. It is good to know that your employer knows your worth**

Last but not least, remember that during the interview you will be encouraged to ask questions. Never allow this opportunity to pass you without asking questions. Here are a few good questions you may ask if you do not already know the answer.

- **What are you looking for in an ideal candidate for this position?**
- **What is the most challenging task of this position?**
- **Are there any changes coming to this position in the future?**

- **What has been the biggest success of this company in the past year?**
- **Why is this position open?**

To best practice the art of the flip, remember to also flip the interview in the end. Right before you shake hands with the person or person(s) interviewing you. This question seems to always throw off employers and enchant them. Ask them:

Do I have your recommendation for this position?

This is a fair question, you put in time to prepare for their interview, and your time is just as valuable. For the most part you will be met with a response similar to "I can't answer that at this time, but if interested we will be in touch". Don't worry, it was a great way to be memorable and standout.

Chapter Three: The Physical

Sometimes, it's the physical that gets you the interview. One day an elderly client from Tanzania walked into my career center to apply for a job. I asked her, what's your date of birth? She kindly replied November, 1926. 1926! She was 89 years old and looking for a job! We went over her resume, and I got her an interview the same day. She was very appreciative. If I were a hiring manager, I would not hire her for anything that she was incapable of doing; however, her presence gained her favor. **She was just very interesting to interact with.** Maybe she knew that she could play on one's heartstrings and that if she showed initiative she would receive favor, maybe not. Either way it worked.

Sometimes the physical gets you attention, so use it. The Physical covers so much, since so much is said without verbiage. There was once a young man who visited my career center regularly with an arm deformity that affected his handshake. He had the ability to properly grip, but the wrist and hand were bent inward out. He came into the career center every day for guidance and always emphasized that we do a mock interview. **A mock interview is an emulation of an interview used for training purposes.** The interview tries to resemble a real interview as closely as possible. In our interviews I would always find myself encouraging him to sit up straight, he slouched whenever seated, not as a physical need, but as a defense mechanism. He was timid, and it was a big characteristic we had to deal with. It was holding him back.

We practiced his handshake over and over. **We went over properly introducing yourself, with assertiveness and kindness.** To do this one must show enthusiasm when giving a firm handshake. I did have to take into  consideration his hand, and how he could get past it. For him, gripping the fingers worked out better than the entire palm. Eye contact was a problem for him as well.

Eye contact is a huge issue for many people, but it can be the difference between getting the job or not. If you have a problem looking a person in the eye, focus your eyes on the middle of their forehead. The other person will never know the difference. If you suffer from a cross eye like I do, focus on only one eye of the person you are speaking to. The other person will not know the difference. The young man lacked in aggression; he was kind, but kind rarely gets you noticed.

Be polite, but very direct. This is no time to be shy, you only have a few moments to introduce your presence and be received well. I counted every time he said, "like" or "um" and every time I counted ten he would have to re-answer the last answer he gave me to a question. This was the hardest thing for him to overcome. **There is no greater way to weaken you as a candidate that to use the words "um" "like" or phrases like "feel me?" or "know what I'm saying?"** These are distracting, interrupt the flow of the conversation and make you look unaware and incompetent.

Today, try to count every time you say, "um," "like" or anything similar in a ten minute span during your next conversation. You may be surprised at how many times you use this form of speech. Try never to speak like this all together. It is not necessary.

It goes without saying that distractions are a problem in job interviews. Earrings should not make noise, and cell phones should be turned off. Not on vibrate, off. **You should never be at a loss for physical documents. Always have several copies of your resume printed and neatly available.** A briefcase or folder is appropriate to bring into an interview. Again, going back to the premise of being on a date. You would not look prepared if your digging into your pockets for your phone, a piece of gum or your wallet at all times. If its takes three minutes for you to dig in your purse for a napkin, you look unorganized.

  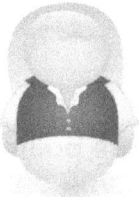

The person makes the clothes but in interviews the clothes can make a person. The general rule of thumb is to match the dress code of the company you are interviewing for and surpass it by one level. In the IT world, most companies allow for slacks comfortable shoes (not sneakers) and polo t-shirts. In an interview in this industry a pair of slacks, hard bottom shoes and a matching tucked in button long sleeve shirt would be one level above that. Let's go over **what you should not be wearing or doing** in a job interview.

Cloths:
- T-Shirts
- Jeans
- Sagging' pants
- Oversized clothes
- Sneakers
- Spaghetti string shirts
- Marinas (Wife Beater, A-shirt, Tank top in some vernacular)
- High heels over one inch
- Sandals and flip Flops
- Sunglasses

Body:
- Men's earrings
- Heavy makeup
- Facial piercing such as lip rings, tongue rings eyebrow rings nose rings.
- Un-brushed or combed hair
- Dirty fingernails
- Distracting fingernail polish
- Chewing gum

Let's go over things **you should be wearing and doing** in a job interview.

Cloths:
- Wear the best in your closet – Be neat and clean, no wrinkles.
- Men: Shirt, tie and collared shirt
- Women: Blouse, Long skirt (below knees), Dress Slacks

- Men: Dress Pants or Khakis
- Women: Low heel shoes (Wedges can also work if they are not sandals)
- Men: Socks that match outfit
- Women: One pair of earrings (Men should not wear earrings, but this is up to you)
- Men: Watches (Worn on the left hand)

Body:
- Hide Tattoos
- Use conservative amount of make up
- Use conservative amount of cologne and perfume (I should only smell you if one foot near you)
- Pins are okay but stay away from religious or political affiliation
- If wearing a suit cufflinks are appropriate if not distracting

Remember to speak clearly, be kind, say hello to everyone at that work site. Practice good posture when sitting or standing, make good eye contact, listen attentively and answer well. **Remember to leave a thank you card with the employer.** This sign of gratitude can be as cheap as 99 cents and creates a memory in the employer's head. **Never leave tangible gifts, that is illegal, because if hired you "gifted" your way into the position. This is a form of Payola.**

Try making a checklist for everything you need on the day of your interview. Here is an example:

- 3 copies of my resume
- Business outfit
- Copy of my application
- Address and Time
- Pen
- Thank you card

Chapter Four: The Hindrance

Hindrance is a thing that provides resistance, delay, or obstruction to something or someone. **We all face some hindrance that is unique to us alone. Some of the time, without even knowing, we mask our hindrance while in the job market.** As a career advisor there was a time, I was serving a single mother who saw me on average three times a week. Each time she came into my career center she had at least one child with her. The only rule I held in my career center was to treat it like a workplace. It was important to get the clients into the mood of the workforce setting. It was also beneficial to have the full attention of the client as to help them the best. Understand their situation, assess it and provide quality assistance. As kind as this mother was, it was hard to help her because she was always distracted by her children. They would yell out and knock over things. They made a lot of noises and created a huge disturbance for her and other people in the career center. How was I suppose to be a good career advisor without her full attention? One day she came into the career center fired up and excited, we were having a hiring event the next day. She allowed me to school her about the company that was hiring and reformat her resume for the job. She was very qualified. However, her children kept interrupting us, **she was not able to focus and much of the information we went over she could not retain.**

The next day at the hiring event she came in dressed professional and with resume in hand. She interviewed and afterward told me that it went well. Later that day I asked the hiring manager about the people she saw that day. Without naming names, she specifically went back to her interview with the mother and explained that she was the best candidate but that she knew very little about the company, and that weakened her chances severely. **Listen, the truth is we all have hardships and shortcomings that we need help with, but these issues are to be kept out of the work arena.** The person that is interviewing you should not have to fight through any distraction to see your **"undeniable factor"**. This factor can be your ability to speak well, your leadership ability; your ease at taking instruction and executing a task.

Whatever it is, it should be easy to see, and nothing should hinder it. **You should always be prepared. Allow nothing should get in the way of that.** There was a gentleman who frequented my career center regularly; he was an extremely fast typist and very mellow guy.
After noticing him for a while, I sat down with him and asked him about his current situation. He

explained to me that he was an ex-college professor and desperate for work but that he could not return to the education arena. I asked why? He broke down and was honest with me. He had slept with one of his students and lost his job, and he had been blacklisted from the educational world. Teaching was out, but he had a lot of transferable skills that made him a great candidate for other jobs. Transferable skills are skills that you can take with you from one situation to another, from one job to another. To add to his hindrance, his wife left him, and he was homeless. This man could speak well, and it was easy to tell that at one time he was well groomed and took care of his family very well. He was in ruin. Eventually, we did a resume, and he started regularly interviewing for different jobs. His spirit was lifted, and he was changing for the better. However, after he and his ex-wife started to communicate again, and he found hope in possibly returning to his family, he picked up the bottle again.

 One day I was leaving the career center, and I saw a body laying on the concrete in 110-degree weather. I walked up to it and saw that it was the ex-professor. I kneeled down beside him and asked if he was alright. He looked red and dehydrated. He said that was okay but that his wife would not take him back. I asked if he was going to hurt himself, and he promised not to. He assured me that he was fine and had a place to sleep that night. Every day after that his spirit weakened again. He got none of the jobs he interviewed for. His undeniable factor was

gone. The hindrance in his life of alcoholism prevented him from finding work.

The truth is in life, you will fall, and that's life. We all have our shortcomings. **Do not let these shortcomings hinder your talent, your charm, your undeniable factor.** That factor alone will carry you in life. Think about your undeniable factor, what several unrelated people like about you the same. What other bosses have noticed in you. Whatever stands out the most, should be what you polish and display the most, because it is natural for you. This verb or short sentence should be on your resume and in your cover letter. For example, if you are magnificent at memorization but think it's a weak skill to display, think again.

Let's say you are going for a job as a customer service representative for inbound calls. In your objective line on a resume or your cover letter, you should write a sentence like this:

Possesses excellent memory and ability to remember clients and their needs on a daily or weekly basis.

The first thing to notice here is that you just flipped a sentence into two part about me section. You told the potential employer that you are good with clients and specifically that you have a great memory. **Great Job, you are mastering the Art of The Flip!**

Chapter Five: The Resume

A lot of times when helping clients create or re-create their resumes I am met with a lot of grief and embarrassment. **People say things like, "I don't have a lot of experiences." or "My work history is too old." or "I'm not qualified for anything."** This is almost never the case and to explain why, I always find myself telling the same one of my favorite jokes.

It comes from *Rush Hour 2* a film starring Chris Tucker and Jackie Chain as a dysfunctional cop duo trying to solve a murder mystery. As the two walk out of the building after uncovering a huge twist, Chris Tucker looks at Jackie Chain and says proudly, "If I keep up this great police work, they gonna' mess around and let me protect the President!" Jackie Chain replies, "But you would never take a bullet for the president!?" Then Chris quickly says, with confidence and charisma and charm "But they don't know that!" That is too funny! I laugh every time, and as I laugh I see the client laugh, and then I ask what does it mean? They never understand how it relates.

How it relates is simple, no one but yourself understands your skills as well as you do. No one but yourself knows how much you are willing to put into a job, no one but yourself understands what your limits are as an employee. Therefore, do not allow your resume to create any limits on you. Never lie on a resume, that we don't even have to go over, it is pointless and eventually catches up with you, but never undermined yourself either.

The truth is, there is no right way to write a resume. There is however a wrong way. Not being clear, a sloppy look and ambiguous approach will not get you noticed or taken seriously. Also, a jack of all trades resume is not a good approach. Again, looking at job interviews as dates, think if you would meet up with someone if their profile says "Looking for a relationship, and maybe to hook up and kids but probably just a date for a wedding my cousin is having"? Probably not, because it is not clear what this person wants. Be clear.

Let us start by taking a look at the factors that makeup Resumes:

What is a Resume?
Your intro letter to the employer, explaining why you are the most or just as competent for the job.

What isn't a Resume?
A list of every job you have ever had ever.

Resume do what?
A resume gets the interview. (Most of the time, sometimes the physical gets you the job.)

What doesn't a Resume do?
Guarantee you a job or interview. Don't be frustrated by this, just be persistent by following up with calls or resending a resume. (Unless you were turned down by a job that does not encourage re-applying). A resume does not replace the application.

Applications Vs. Resumes
An application is a legal document that you have to sign. They ask for information about your criminal history, work history and salary requirements. Resumes don't answer any of that information. You should not list any of this information on your resume. Don't ruin your chances by being that forward on your resume. Let's go over what not to put on your resume to make it most effective:

Listing your entire work history.
Only list relevant jobs that you are applying for with this resume.

Listing expected pay.
You don't want to turn off a potential employer by looking over qualified or inexperienced.

Listing personal information.
Information such as age, race, religion, or sexual orientation.

When writing the resume, the biggest things you want to emphasize is how valuable you are, and **you show that you are valuable with the small details.** The salt & pepper, a little salt, a little pepper.

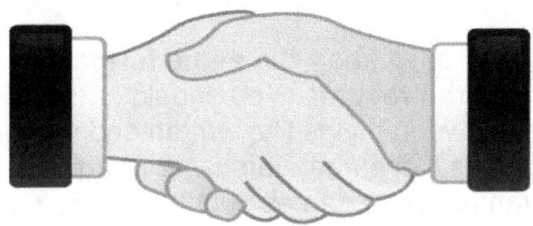

Even if you are going for a job at a movie theater as an usher for a minimum wage, emphasize that you are a professional by using proper grammar thinking wisely about your word choice. You should avoid using 'I' and 'You'. Write in 3rd person. For example, a description of a job on one's resume for cashier should not read:

"I worked the register and greeted guest. I helped placed back on shelves lost goods, and I cashed out my drawer each night."

Instead, it should be written in 3rd person and be worded like this:

"Operated cash register and greeted guest in store. Helped during slow hours by placing back on shelves scattered goods. Assisted manager by cashing out my register each night."

A lot of word processing programs will give you the green line for incorrect grammar. However, while typing the resume, it is important to use 3rd person throughout the entire resume.

According to Merriam-Webster Dictionary 3rd person is: a set of words or forms (such as pronouns or verb forms) that refer to people or things that the speaker or writer is not addressing directly.

Remember to keep the same formatting throughout the resume. You should not switch back and forth between things like written and numeric dates such as December versus 12 or abbreviated and written out state names such as NY versus New York. I recommend avoiding abbreviations altogether. It is much more formal to spell out each word such as street versus St. the funny thing is, it is very easy to misspell, and abbreviates words like, etc. think about how many time you have misspelled as ect. Remember "Big up your damn self!" That is what the presentation of your resume is all about.

Let's now go over the different sections of a Resume.

First you have the Heading

A heading should appear on all of the pages you send an employer; it should be the same heading for the cover letter (we will go over) and resume. If the resume is longer than a page, include the header on the other pages as well. The Heading should include your full legal Name (no nicknames). Your best contact phone number (no more than two). Your professional Email address (Nothing like lilyunghot68@world.com) in all seriousness, if your email sound like this, get a new one. Lastly, the heading should include your address. In my opinion, you do not have to include "mi·nute" details about your address such as address and apartment number, but the city and state are crucial. The application asks for your exact address. If you don't have to throw your address around town, don't.

The Objective

Every resume you make needs to have an objective to let the employer know what you want and why you are a good hire. The objective is a quick read never more than four sentences. Use this section to tell the employer politely your worth, what you are willing to do and the position you are looking for. If your resume does not name a specific job title, it should at least indicate the type of work you're interested in. Here are a few examples of good objectives.

"Ten year plus experienced Video Editor skilled in Adobe Premiere and Final Cut Pro (6 - X) and Videographer seeking to use skills on a growing and dynamic team."

"Developed customer service associate employing verbal and written bilingual abilities in English and Swahili looking for a position on a sales team."

"Talented and motivated team leader seeking to secure an entry level position as a Customer Service Representative in a local call center."

"Pursuing a career as a Customer Service Representative benefiting from over five years of related experience while displaying a caring, helpful attitude; a desire to teach and inform; and a never-ending curiosity about what's going on around myself; On a team with advancement opportunities."

Using action verbs spice up one's objective. **Action verbs are words that show any action. They express things about a person can do.** I also suggest describing yourself using an interesting noun. Nouns are often described as referring to persons, places, things, states, or qualities so why not make an interesting quality. Words like; talented, skilled, experienced and bilingual are examples of interesting nouns.

The Qualifications

These are bullet list skills and traits that you have, and employers want. These should appear under or after your objective and give support to your objective. If a skill you list does not support your objective, take it out. For Example:

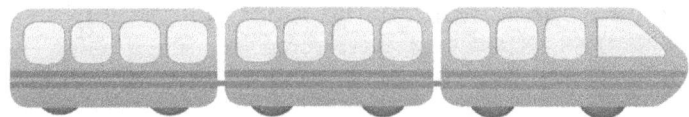

"Ten year plus experienced Video Editor skilled in Adobe Premiere and Final Cut Pro (6 - X) and Videographer seeking to use skills on a growing and dynamic team."

- Possesses extensive know-how of video editing and shooting styles
- Excellent ability to work with others, interview participants and record high-quality audio.
- Ability to accurately highlight and depicts events and culture in video production
- Excellent dishwashing skills

Dishwashing skills? What does dishwashing have to do with any of this? It just weakened the resume.

Work History

Work History is experience you list to show an employer that you are a stable employee. It also can exemplify that you have done similar work in the past. The descriptions of your work history should always relate to your objective. This is another way to flip the situation and appeal more to the employer. The general rule of thumb is that you don't go back past ten years of work history. However, if you have gaps in your employment and need to, it is acceptable. Also, if the related work in your field goes back ten years, then it will be necessary to list it on your resume because it is relevant. At the same time remember, you are not listing every single job you ever had.

Keep in mind that gaps of time look bad to employers. They instantly think you were in jail, or were too lazy to work. No matter what your situation was, think very hard about the tasks you did for money or volunteer. Baby sitting, helping at your local church, taking care of an ill family member. These are not just things that have the word job attached to them. Work history is work history; they are to be treated as such.

Education

This section of the resume scares a lot of people on both sides of the spectrum. Those that are very educated and those who have received little education. The point of this section is to show the employer what you know book wise. It can show that you care about self-empowerment and improvement. I suggest that you list all of your education, if you come across as overly qualified, you are. Excluding some of my education on my resume for a job never worked for me. On the flip side, let's say you do not have a GED. I suggest you get one, find a free or low-cost program and earn it from an accredited institution as soon you can do it. The graduation date on the resume does not have to be in the past. The completion date can be listed as well. If you are not enrolled in a program look into a program and write down that programs completion date if you plan to enroll. At the same time, remember that education is optional, it does not have to be put down, but I recommend it. If relevant do not be afraid to but down college course, workshops, seminars and training courses. Even if they are not related to the field you are applying for because it shows you as an achiever, with a go-getter personality. Even if it was a comic con writers workshop, show that you have an active and proactive mind and that you are not just a reactive person merely existing.

Accomplishments

This is an optional section and allows you to mention any time you went above and beyond your job description for a customer or your organization, or both! A time when you excelled in your job, and were recognized for positive reasons. This can be awards and achievements or the completion of courses and training. **Remember, "Big up your damn self!**

One key thing to note is that after the heading and objective, the resume can be put into any order. Make it clean, make it unique and make it good. In the next few pages are examples of good resumes that all were used to get clients jobs. Study them and use the format to create your resume.

John Doe Palmer
123 W. Main Street
San Francisco, California
(562) 555 4523
Jaypalmer@world.com

OBJECTIVE

Pursuing a career as a Customer Service Representative benefiting from over five years of related experience while displaying a caring, helpful attitude; a desire to teach and inform; and a never-ending curiosity about what's going on around me; on a team with advancement opportunities.

QUALIFICATIONS

- Answered a high volume of telephone calls from customers regarding accounts and processes
- Maintained contact and followed up on problems that required special handling
- Provided support by making outbound calls for special promotions and events
- Researched and responded to customer inquiries and explained transactions to their satisfaction
- Recognized by clients who appreciated my extra efforts
- Assisted clients in the selection of products
- Providing appropriate help and advice by writing careers literature, action plans and reports.
- Proficient in use of specialized computer applications
- Possesses plenty of confidence and excellent listening, verbal and written communication skills.

EMPLOYMENT

| Febuary 2014 to Present | **Duvey Career Center** *Career Advisor* | San Francisco, California |

Explored and evaluated the clients education, training, work history, interests, skills, and personality traits. Arranged for aptitude and achievement tests to help the client make career decisions. Assisted individuals with career decisions. Worked with individuals to develop their job-search skills and assist clients in locating and applying for jobs. Provided career counseling. Provided support to people experiencing job loss, job stress, or other career transition issues.

| May 2014 to Present | **JNC Films** *Video Editor* | San Francisco, California |

Watch scenes and determine which will end up on cutting room floor. Rearrange scenes. Work with and manipulate raw camera footage, dialogue, sound effects, graphics and special effects. Determine which camera angles to use. Insert music, sound, and optical effects. Delivered edited timeline project in Adobe Premiere Pro along with finalization notes and music used.

| February 2014 to August 2014 | **KTVL - FriscoFamily Network** *Studio Technician* | San Francisco, California |

Assist in the production of live newscasts, during special events and for taped programming. Call up teleprompter scripts. Write news briefs for online content. Operate TelePrompter video switcher on live air. Work closely with Directors and Producers to ensure optimal production.

The Art of the Flip: How to creatively succeed in Job Interviews

John Doe Palmer
123 W. Main Street
San Francisco, California
(562) 555 4523
Jaypalmer@world.com

EDUCATION

January 2012
Savannah, Georgia

Savannah College of Art and Design

M.F.A. - Film And Television Production

The development process of film and television. Securing the
rights to creative material. Film and television financing,
Organizing, budgeting and scheduling productions. Marketing,
distribution and exhibition.

May 2009
Raleigh, North Carolina

Shaw University

Broadcast Journalism

Developed ability to understand and synthesize ideas into a
message someone else can use, and strong verbal and writing
skills. Broadcast news writing, videography and editing,
television reporting and producing, mass communication law.

Jamie Brown
2100 West Obie Ave – New York, New York
980-555-1998 - 980-555-2327 - **Jamieb@world.com**

OBJECTIVE

Pursuing a career as a Warehouse Clerk employing verbal and written bilingual abilities in English and Spanish and over 6 years of experience.

QUALIFICATIONS

- Experienced at loading and unloading products
- Able move and lift over 50lbs. frequently.
- Picked, packed and shipped orders.
- Relocated products using forklifts, reach lifts and pallet jacks.
- Able to quickly and safely complete tasks.
- Processing paperwork and labeling merchandise.
- Computer literate and have knowledge of MS Windows.
- Able to work in adverse conditions including high temperatures, high noise levels and moving mechanical parts.

CERTIFICATION

Forklift License - OSHA: Construction Safety & Health
Certificate of Basic Carpentry - Certificate of Foundations of Construction

EMPLOYMENT

September 2004 -   Mortgage Investors   New York, New York
June 2005   ***Appointment Setter***
Delivered prepared sales talks that describe products and services in order to persuade potential customers to lower their mortgage. Explained products, services, and prices, and answered questions from customers. Recorded names, addresses, purchases and reactions of prospects contacted.

January 2002 -   Complete Sky Cap Service   Newark, New Jersey
August 2004   ***Airport Sky Cap/Customer Service***
Met passengers as they arrive with especially heavy luggage. Assist with wheelchairs, strollers, and oversized items. Performed curbside check-ins for flights. Helped unload luggage from cars and taxis. Answered questions from passengers and family members.

October 1997 -   Allen Dawn Corp   Worcester, Massachusetts
January 2002   ***Dispatch/Driver***
Scheduled and dispatched workers, work crews, equipment, and service vehicles to appropriate locations using radios or telephones. Relayed work orders, messages, and information to or from work crews, supervisors, and field inspectors. Arranged for necessary repairs to restore furniture. Excellent safety record, Delivered, loaded and unloaded goods. Performed various task using hand track and dolly. Collected payments and obtained receipts for goods. Inspected all goods.

February 1994 -   Kaye Inc.   Tempe, Arizona
September 1997   ***Customer Service / Lead man***
Supervised the activities of workers engaged in receiving, storing, testing, and shipping products or materials. Conferred with department heads to coordinate warehouse activities. Assisted all customers who came to warehouse for pickups.

EDUCATION

June 1998   **Phoenix Department Of Education**,   Phoenix, Arizona   *G.E.D.*

Nicole Noel Clark
Bellflower, California 90706
562.555.1888 - Noel.Nicole@world.com

OBJECTIVE

Actively pursuing a career as a Airline Stewardess benefiting from over five years of related aviation experience.

QUALIFICATIONS

- Answered a high volume of telephone calls from customers regarding payments, returns and charges to accounts
- Maintained contact and followed up on problems that required special handling
- Provided marketing support by making outbound sales calls for special promotions
- Researched and responded to customer inquiries and explained transactions to their satisfaction
- Recognized by customers who appreciated my extra efforts
- Maintained close liaison with customers on issues relating to bookings. Managed database and back office as required. Ensured all issues relating to ticketing complied with best practice.
- Monitored and communicated airline schedule changes and flight cancellations. Checked all manifests against information booked.

CERTIFICATION

Computer skills: Word - PowerPoint - Excel Typing: 40 wpm – Air Hostess training program – CPR Card

EMPLOYMENT

November 2008 to March 2013	**JetGreen Airways** *Airport/Ground Operations*	Long Beach, California

Worked well to achieve targets and ensured that all queues and updates were regularly checked. Utilized all preferred Airline contacts. Assigned flights to the cruise system and ensured that allocations were used. Handled internal and external calls, offering the highest level of customer service. Issued airline tickets for bookings in line with contracts. Check-in customers and make travel reservations.

October 2007 to June 2008	**Devy Creamery** *Ice Cream Preparer/Cashier*	Long Beach, California

Prepared ice cream for customers in store and through telephone orders. Customized ice cream cakes for special occasions. Operated the cash register and balanced totals daily.

November 2004 to June 2006	**JC Dime – Lakewood Mall** *Customer Service Representative:*	Lakewood, California

Provided customer service and organized merchandize. Managed cash register and prepared passengers and aircraft for landing following procedures.

EDUCATION

January 2008 Cerritos, California	**Cerritos College** *Broadcast Journalism*

June 2006 Long Beach, California	**Juan Rodriguez Cabrillo High School** *Diploma*

Veronica Parkinson - Lopez

Mesa, Arizona
602.555.4664
Parkinson.love7@world.com

OBJECTIVE

Motivated High School student pursuing a position as a customer service associate employing verbal and written bilingual abilities in English and Swahili.

Accomplishments

Captain of Volleyball team at Peter Central High School – 3.4 GPA – Student of the year – Perfect attendance recipient.

QUALIFICATIONS

* Supported children emotional and social development
* Sanitized toys and play equipment
* Disciplined children and recommend other measures to control behavior
* Observed and monitored children play
* Kept records on individual children
* Instructed children in health and personal habits
* Organized and participated in recreational activities such as games

EMPLOYMENT

March 20011 to Present
Independent Child Sitter
Phoenix, Arizona
Sitter
Control & care for kids at the employer's residence. Prepare bottles and snacks for infants and children respectively. Bathe, dress and groom infants and children. Arrange formulas and change diapers. Teach basic language and math lessons. Organize and take part in leisure activities such as games, crafts, comics, outings and exercise. Discipline children in keeping with the methods requested by the parents. Maintain a clean and healthy environment inside the home. Keep an eye on children's activities.

March 2009 to Present
Sacred Mountain Temple Church of Christ
Phoenix, Arizona
Activity Volunteer
Assisted in the coordination and planning of fund raising activities. Interacted with public and promoted agency programs and events. Organized agency files and maintained records of contributions.

EDUCATION

Class of May 2016

Peter Central High School   **Phoenix, Arizona**

The Art of the Flip: How to creatively succeed in Job Interviews

Gregory D. Moore
62. N. Vern Ln. - Phoenix, Arizona 85003
610 555 3281 - Gmoore45@world.com

OBJECTIVE

Seeking a challenging and productive position in Broadcast utilizing over 15 years of Radio and Television broadcasting with extensive floor Direction experience.

QUALIFICATIONS

Report news stories for publication or broadcast, describing the background and details of events.
Arrange interviews with people who can provide information about a story
Review copy and correct errors in content, grammar, and punctuation, following prescribed editorial style and formatting guidelines.
Determine a story's emphasis, length, and format, and organize material accordingly.
Operate television or motion picture cameras to record scenes for television broadcasts, advertising, or motion pictures.
Compose and frame each shot, applying the technical aspects of light, lenses, film, filters, and camera settings to achieve the sought look.
Up to date AVID Editor. Ability to edit video for broadcast production.
Prepare and deliver Radio news, sports, or weather reports, gathering and rewriting material so that it will convey required information and fit specific time slots.
Read news flashes to inform audiences of important events.
Identify stations, and introduce or close shows, using memorized or read scripts, and/or ad-libs.

CERTIFICATION

Television Engineering   Society of Broadcast Engineering

EMPLOYMENT

01 / 1990 to
Phoenix, Arizona
Present

Clean Comedy.com

Professional Comedian
Collaborate with other actors as part of an ensemble. Perform humorous and serious interpretations of emotions, actions, and situations, using body movements, facial expressions, and gestures.

01 / 2003 to
Scottsdale, Arizona
08 / 2008

Scottsdale Airpark News

Contributing Writer
Research and report on the specialized field of business, created review segments to inform and entertain viewers. Segments had a demographic audience of 30,000 viewers.

01 / 2003 to
Phoenix, Arizona
06 / 2008

KNPX NEWS 12

Floor Director
Knowledge of media production, communication, and dissemination techniques and methods. This includes alternative ways to inform and entertain via written, oral, and visual media. Assign operators to cameras and direct talent to which cameras were on.

03 / 1997 to	**KYET Radio**
Williams, Arizona	
05 / 2003	*Station Manager*

Plan and schedule programming and event coverage, based on broadcast length, time availability, and other factors, such as community needs, ratings data, and viewer demographics. Coordinate activities between departments, such as news and programming. Direct and coordinate activities of personnel engaged in broadcast news, sports, or programming. Monitor and review programming to ensure that schedules are met, guidelines are adhered to, and performances are of adequate quality.

05 / 1990 to	**KWBF TV-13**
Flagstaff, Arizona	
09 / 1997	*Public Service Director*

Develop ideas for programs and features that a station could produce. Prepare copy and edit tape so that material is ready for broadcasting. Establish work schedules and assign work to staff members. Traveled to several different cities to produce broadcast quality segment based show.

EDUCATION

Milwaukee, Wisconsin

Institute Of Broadcast Arts

Radio Broadcasting
Vocational Diploma

Cardinal Stritch College
Milwaukee, Wisconsin
Study of Sociology

REFRENCES

Tom Doe	Daily Sun Newspaper	Flagstaff, AZ.	(989) 555-5527
Brahm Jane Doe	KPNX TV-12	Phoenix, AZ.	(621) 555-5512
Andrew Drake	Phoenix Video Prod.	Mesa, AZ.	(418) 555-5591

Greg's resume is interesting in that it break some rules. North and Lane are abbreviated in the header. The header is not on both pages, and there are references listed on the actual resume. However, this resume landed this client a very well paying job. The client understood better than I what those in his field were looking for. I was merely the machine that bottled it all together and put it into nice wrapping. Sometimes the conventional ways of doing the resume will not apply to your situation. But this is a good foundation to base your resume on.

Kevin J. Parkinson

Close:

   What we have learned is the value to overstand the flip, the physical, the hindrance and the resume. Overstanding is the ability to perceive the unseen or the unexplained; it is this characteristic that brings us answers that unlock the door of acceptance. The flip is the ability to turn distracting questions into favorable answers. Every answer in the interview should be met with appealing information about you as an employee. It is imperative to keep two to three fascinating stories about times you went above and beyond the call of duty for your organization or customer. These stories sale you as a valuable employee. The physical is the attributes you use to consciously and subconsciously gain favor and create intrigue from the employer. The hindrance is the issues we all face that can to detrimental to our job search. While still handling our responsibilities, we must not allow hindrance to distract us or keep us from gaining employment. The Resume is often our first introduction to a potential employer. It is important that it is thoroughly made and sales you as the best for the position you are applying for.

   If you have made it this far in the book, I appreciate you reading. I hope the information shared in this book brings much success your way. Whether this is your first job, dream job or that BIG job you have been hoping for. I wanted to leave you with a new way to think, a new perspective. No matter how hard it may get, remember to live for tomorrow. Ask yourself, will this tattoo hurt me tomorrow? Will this DUI hurt me tomorrow? Will this domestic disturbance hurt me tomorrow? Will this website get me into

44

trouble? Will having this substance on me get me into trouble? As a career advisor, I have witnessed countless times these things hurt people looking for work. Some still go on to find gainful employment, but most are held back, due to a record or one bad decision. You are a brand, just a valuable as Nike or Apple.

Protect your brand at all cost; because when it's time to make your brand work for you, you don't want anything affecting your chances or earning the most possible. Try and remember, there is no perfect suit to wear, no perfect resume to have and no perfect handshake. However, there is a right way of doing things. That way changes as culture and society changes but one thing remains the same, and that is class. Have a class about the way you present yourself. Other than that, everything works differently for everybody, use the tools in this book to enhance yourself and work for you. Be the best brand the employer in your next interview has ever come across.

Big up your damn self!

ABOUT THE AUTHOR

Kevin J. Parkinson is an accomplished Career Advisor, Writer and Film Maker. Kevin was born in Mt. Vernon New York to immigrant parents from Jamaica. The family moved to Los Angeles where Kevin grew up. He Attended Bellflower High School, and enrolled into Cerritos College at the age of 16. After High School he attended Mt. San Antonio College then transferred to Shaw University in Raleigh North Carolina. He earned his Masters degree from The Savannah College of Art and Design. When Kevin returned home from college he found himself with many skills but was being turned down regularly for positions he  was qualified for. He developed his "flip" method and was able to land a position as a career advisor for the Goodwill of Southern California. Kevin was later offered a position within the Goodwill of Central Arizona and at the printing of this book is still there, teaching the art of the flip. Kevin now resides with his wife in Phoenix, Arizona.